T0116484

ON THE HEALER'S JOURNEY

Coaching Book for Seekers

EDIT B KISS

BALBOA.PRESS

A DIVISION OF HAY HOUSE

Balboa Press books may be ordered through booksellers or by contacting:

Balboa Press
A Division of Hay House
1663 Liberty Drive
Bloomington, IN 47403
www.balboapress.com
844-682-1282

Because of the dynamic nature of the Internet, any web addresses or
links contained in this book may have changed since publication and
may no longer be valid. The views expressed in this work are solely those
of the author and do not necessarily reflect the views of the publisher,
and the publisher hereby disclaims any responsibility for them.

The author of this book does not dispense medical advice or prescribe the use
of any technique as a form of treatment for physical, emotional, or medical
problems without the advice of a physician, either directly or indirectly. The
intent of the author is only to offer information of a general nature to help
you in your quest for emotional and spiritual well-being. In the event you use
any of the information in this book for yourself, which is your constitutional
right, the author and the publisher assume no responsibility for your actions.

Any people depicted in stock imagery provided by Getty Images are
models, and such images are being used for illustrative purposes only.
Certain stock imagery © Getty Images.

Print information available on the last page.

ISBN: 979-8-7652-2951-4 (sc)
ISBN: 979-8-7652-2952-1 (e)

Balboa Press rev. date: 06/29/2022

To my children Krisztian and Eszter
for being my biggest supporters
To my mother who always had my back
To my amazing friends who believed in me

Reviews

"Thank you for writing a book that encourages to discover the magnificent way of energies. I really felt while reading that you claim every word with your healing path. Samadhi meditation is the best meditation I recently tried. Thank you for sharing it with us!

Since earliest childhood I feel people's energy (it always turned out it was true), I see and feel life through my heart chakra and finally my profession is classical music (opera singer and vocal coach). I Chanell music all the time. The story about Egypt was a big surprise, because I visited that country 3 times and stayed every time for three weeks, and it happened 2,3 years before I started meditating, and I felt while walking in Alexandria that I must have lived here ages ago, a very grounded feeling. Of course, my mom looked at me with a very strange look....

While reading I felt that my discoveries are not finished. I'd like to wide my knowledge to first clean up myself thoroughly. Thank you one more time!

As you said, you never know who will bring you to whom and in which ways, very happy to meet you in this lifetime.

Please, write more books!"

Ida Kani

"I read your book, and it was awesome! Many Aha moments for me. I have to say it is a Great book, guide. I read it in a short time, and it was enjoyable. Very interesting descriptions and examples. Very understandable, giving straightforward, complete, immediate answers, without "sauces". It is pleasant, interesting, great content, useful guide, for those of us that we feel we are walking in the same path of the light, of love, of offering and of feeling our healing power. I identified with many points you describe, and the explanations are simple to understand for our minds and hearts. Very interesting and important part for our protection. Thank you for giving me the opportunity to read it. It was enlightening in many points for me. Everything happens for a reason.

Love and blessings"

***Gloria Lagopoulou ***

"I really enjoyed Edit's book "On The Healer's Journey" I found her stories to be very relatable and validating. If you feel called as a Lightworker, then this book is for you. It breaks down simple steps of understanding and knowing to embodying and becoming. Get a copy today to help you on your journey!"

Kat Moulton

"Edit's background and unique perspective and experiences have given her extraordinary insight into spiritual growth for herself and for others. I enjoyed reading about her personal experiences and thorough research to be able to serve and lead others to heal and maintain a high vibration throughout life. As a fellow coach with a different foundation, I see the practical value of learning from Edit."

Gina T Coach

"Thank you for the book, I have had the chance to read it. It's an awesome book and reflects the healer's journey well although many of the references/ terms used were new and alien to me. One very important comment I noticed - even though your book relates to healing and light workers, it applies to everyone going through life's transformation. I am seeking to leave my 9-5 job into online business and most of the things you mentioned I have/ am experiencing."

Tafi

"This is incredible thank you so much! I have until now felt so alone on this journey, but I resonated with every single word in this book that I no longer feel that way! I have been in the dark so long and been feeling the pain until the last 6 months I've been telling my family I think I was an Egyptian queen in a last life, and I have been having some incredible experiences since this!!! But until now I thought I was crazy."

Emma Owen

"Firstly, thank you for letting me read your book. I found it very insightful and a lot of what you wrote resonated with me (especially when you mentioned New Zealand as I was born there). I liked the way you explained your own journey and your change. I love the easy-to-read structure of the chapters and they are filled with just enough information. Very easy to take in I think this will be a very beneficial tool for helping Light workers find their own power and I am excited to see the final product. Thank you so much"

Richard Melrose

Contents

Introduction

Welcome to my coaching book. Lately, I have met several people who are either struggling to accept that they are a lightworker, or they are on the beginner phase and are still not fully aligned and aware of the key elements to proceed safely on this path.

In this book I will provide information, mindfulness, and spiritual tools to make your life easier through this process. How to identify where you are in the process, what you are meant to do on Earth and most importantly how to protect yourself in your sensitive position so you can fully provide your gift to others. Plus, many more fascinating facts about what being a lightworker means to me.

I was also in this situation for years. Firstly, I completed my Reiki certificates to help myself and my family and still I was not following the messages within me. Then, when eventually I quit my life in the corporate world, burned out and with residual mental illness from the past,

I subconsciously created a family retreat in New Zealand for 7 months where I spent most of my time healing myself and enjoying quality time with my family.

That was when I started to have a desire to heal people as a business, as a career, but I was scared to start due to legal issues and only being a tourist in the country. Even though we were under the immigration process to get a residential status once I obtained an engineering position, God had other plans.

I am originally from Hungary, from a small town called Törökszentmiklós, which means Turkish Saint Michael. I really think I have Turkish blood in me from the historical invasion of our country. I always loved traveling to new countries and experiencing new cultures, climates and cuisines. I consider myself a cosmopolitan after living in 8 countries and visiting about 25 altogether.

I was always a dreamer in both contexts. I have had vivid dreams for as long as I can remember; I feel like I have another life whilst I am sleeping. I also like to dream big. Whenever I start something, I want to be the best, or at least very good at it. If I find I do not have the attitude, character or skill needed after doing it for a while, I turn to an exciting new endeavour. I need the inspiration to act.

Before the knowing

Before the knowing

Many of us have no idea that we are going to be a lightworker in our adulthood. Some of us have known since early childhood and simply thought that everyone is capable of what we are: to see and feel spirits, to see the future, to sense the illnesses, to see the auras, to hear the whispers. Some of these gifted people were labelled as stupid or mentally ill and thought better to forget and push back these extra senses.

I was an extremely introverted kid with vivid dreams as I mentioned earlier. I did not know for a long time that this is actually an indication for deep spiritual connection and calling. If you were a kid who loved nature and animals, were caring and kind, that also shows your direction towards this path. We lightworkers, all have had many lives and, on many occasions, we were healers, witches, nuns, priests or priestesses. Before we were born, we knew what our mission in this lifetime would be.

The following information might shock you and I haven't shared it on any media platform yet. Most likely you will have heard of Egyptian mythology and might even be drawn to it. I believe most of the mythologies are true or at least 50% of them. I am sure you are aware that there is only one God/Universe/supreme pure consciousness. So, who were all those gods and goddesses in the mythologies of many cultures? They were extra-terrestrials who were the mentors, masters and guides of the human species. Probably you remember that they were able to die, they would sometimes kill each other and for this reason, they could not be gods. So, what happened to their consciousness, their spirit after they died? They got stuck in the spirit net of the Earth, could not return to their solar system and planet, but also could not be reborn with their vast number of supernatural powers into a human body. That is why they were divided into many consciousness.

Currently on Earth there are many Isis consciousness, Horus consciousness and Osiris consciousness running around. Maybe one of them is you. I will tell you how to find out. For example, I met a lady who is the girlfriend of one of my clients and after the event I started to see her in my meditations, and I felt sisterhood feelings towards her from another planet. I also had the deep knowing that she was the incarnation of Cleopatra, the famous queen in ancient

Egypt. I asked her once how she feels about Egypt and if she is interested in its history and in Cleopatra. She told me that she is studying Cleopatra in depth, is fascinated with her and admired her greatly. She has visited Egypt several times and it has always felt like home to her. That was profound proof for all my hypotheses. Also, she carries many traits and skills of Cleopatra: she speaks 7 languages and her walk and pose are really royal.

Cleopatra started to believe after a certain age that she was Isis. Obviously, some people believed her, some did not, but I am pretty sure she was one of the Isis consciousness of that era and now this lady carries her soul, not knowing her full potential yet. The funny thing is that when I was 16, I used an Egyptian prediction book in which I could ask questions from different "gods" about my life and by pointing my finger on the page with closed eyes, I had an answer. I was just playing, and I did not know what I was doing obviously. I was communicating with my higher self.

I grew up in a communist country, where my parents, being members of the socialist party, were not allowed to go to church. Even though they grew up in a Christian environment and regularly went to church as children, after the Second World War, things changed in the Eastern Block. Religion wasn't a subject discussed at school or at home. When I was in my teenage years, I loved history and mythology and started to read books about different religions. I thought I might pick one after figuring out which is more aligned with my beliefs. Taoism was one religion that I felt comfortable with. It acknowledges a universal central power with which we all can connect and withdraw information, that everything is connected, there is no separation.

Now I know that all religions have parts which align with the known universal laws and scientific facts about energy and its nature. I am a Reiki Master. Reiki originated from Buddhist monks and was created by Usui, a Japanese doctor. I am also a Karma yogi, which originated from Hinduism and has been practised in Kashmir for 60 000 years. I am a certified Sekhem healer; Sekhem healing was established in ancient Egypt many thousands of years ago. As you see I believe we do not need to pick a religion, we were born spiritual and able to connect to God without outside help, so we can find the techniques and tools to heal ourselves and others in the most sufficient way naturally.

Being misunderstood

Being misunderstood

I am assuming that people around you looked at you strangely when you said to them that you want to be a lightworker or a spiritual healer. Maybe you are still afraid to share this with those around you and are hiding whilst reading this book. I understand, we like to be in peace, we do not want to experience confrontation which is perfectly fine. I know it is frustrating that you can't share it with people you love and are deeply connected to. But it could be possible that this assumption is only in your head and if they really love you, they will understand. Even more so if you explain that you want to learn about it because you want to help them too when they are sick. When you share it with them it could also be a test of how much they really care about your passions and desires. On what level they are supportive? As we start our spiritual journey, we start to raise our frequency through meditation, spiritual practises and using crystals. Those around you can be encouraged to follow but some may choose to remain on a low vibration. As lightworkers one of our responsibilities is to help people to raise their vibration. Not everybody is ready for this. Some may not have had past lives. Some have no connection to their higher selves. The best way to make them understand is to gather some information about the topic that demonstrates scientific proof of how certain energy works. If you feel extreme resistance from certain people towards your intention of being a light-worker, you need to re-evaluate that relationship. Is everything else in the relationship fine beside this one point? Or is there other evidence of unhappiness already? If yes it might be the time to set free and heal yourself first before you get involved into another romantic relationship, so you attract the right people. It can also happen to friendships. You can outgrow them due to having different values and interests.

We are spiritual beings having a human experience and we are fully supported. We are co-creators with God so we can manifest whatever we want even new friends. If a negative situation is happening with wider family members, who do not share a home with us anymore such as a mother, brother, or sister you can just give them time away and limit the conversation to different subjects for a while. We do not want to cause karmic debts by being disrespectful towards them. As soon as you make a living out of being a successful spiritual healer, they will probably admire you and ask you for guidance.

What is my path?

What is my path?

I can imagine that you still have a 9–5 job and are working for a paycheck that is hardly enough for your bills and expenses or perhaps you are a successful CEO who has the wealth but not the health and happiness. Maybe you are already out of the workforce and living in a camper van and have no clue what to do with your life.

Whatever category you represent you need to find your way to becoming a lightworker. Sometimes we do not know what our goal is because everything is so difficult, and we can't see clearly. We are mistaking the goal of our ego with the goal of our spirit. When we are at work, we are just climbing the career ladder and we think that is our goal. But that is only a temporary duty in a workplace not our purpose or mission, especially if we feel sick and tired all the time and not excited about what we do.

So first, evaluate what you feel about your current goals (if you have them). Are they aligned with your heart's desire or are you just fulfilling the social expectation of your environment?

To find your path, you need to see your future with your third eye as clearly as you see your present and to know as confidently as you know what you are doing in the next minute. How do you activate your extra sense, your 6th sense, by activating your third eye? There are many ways.

When I was practising Reiki, I was trained to use my extra sense by my Reiki Master and I was able to transmit images of one object through another person or feelings of another person to my mind.

Let's clarify now what the mind is and what the parts of it are. The mind is not in your brain, it is in your whole body, in your senses. It has 4 main parts: the conscious mind, the subconscious mind, the unconscious mind and the superconscious mind. We use the conscious mind about 5% of the time to make a decision and take action. The subconscious mind represents about 45 % of our thoughts and actions, and the unconscious mind is a couple of percentage of the subconscious mind while the superconscious responsible for about 50% of our reactions and responses.

It is really important to understand the functions of the different parts. We use the conscious mind when we set goals, analyse something or focus on a new activity and we can't make any mistakes. The rest of the time we use our subconscious mind for automated behaviours so the body can save energy. Such as when we drive to the shop, brush our teeth, read or cook, things we have done so many times before. But how we do those things or the way we do things depends on our values, belief system, habits, fears and memories which are stored in our subconscious mind. And obviously, you have a bigger chance of making mistakes when you use the subconscious mind instead of being present and using your conscious mind. That is why it is highly recommended to use different routes to the shop or office, try to cook new dishes, be present when you read and fully enjoy what you do. Choose things you enjoy then you will be more present.

The unconscious mind holds the shame, the guilt, the grief, the emotional traumas buried deeply so you won't have conscious access to them, but they make your life miserable by triggers.

Your superconscious mind connects you with your spiritual body and the Universe, such as your higher self, soul family field and planets. That is why seeking information in the field of astrology and numerology helps to understand why we act in a certain way at given times.

Even though through Reiki I had some nice extra sense experiences, it did not move me closer to truly knowing my purpose.

So, let's activate that third eye so you will see your path! The Samadhi meditation was, for me, the first transcendental meditation experience. It is deeper and more powerful than other transcendental meditations I tried. It instantly drags you into the Karma vortex by activating all your 8 chakras. That's right not just the 7 that are in your physical body, but also the 8th chakra which is the soul star chakra and outside of your body. It is the chakra of your aura which holds all your karmic history, achievements, and failures.

When you activate your 8th chakra you will be able to see and find out more about your past lives and understand more fully your purpose. You will receive messages in weird situations. It will make you so sure of your path that you will start to act on it, as it is already yours. That is when the manifestation magic starts happening too. Beside the chakra activation we activate our pineal gland too during this meditation, which brings our brain into delta brainwaves. At this point our brain will start to produce more of the necessary hormones.

Where is me?

Where is me?

Usually, we get dragged along by life so much that we forget about ourselves whilst serving and making others happy. In this chapter I emphasize the importance to please yourself, find the way to celebrate and feel grateful.

As you focus more on using your conscious mind, you can finally see what activities frustrate you and do not make you happy and what circumstances are blocking your happiness. Obviously, you can make yourselves happy and grateful in any condition using your mind, but that would not bring growing and learning. As soon as you get into the Karma vortex it won't be possible to feel fulfilled until you complete your duty, your purpose of this lifetime.

Now start to change how you live. Remember, everything is possible, we are co-creators with God. I will tell you 2 short stories to prove this to you.

When I was overwhelmed in my 9–5, I wished to work only 2 days in the office and spend the rest of the days at home. I said it out loud once in the kitchen before I quit. A couple of months later when I returned from New Zealand, I was able to continue to provide work for my previous company but as a contractor only showing up in the office 2 times a week, making more money and spending more time with my children. So, my wish came true. What happened in New Zealand? Lots of healing with the strongest Reiki Master Signs attracted positive energies to manifest my wish. Having more time and a happier life, I started to learn about digital marketing and realised that I was living in a box. A petroleum engineer box. I hardly had any knowledge about any other industries or other income streams beside my profession. I realised I was missing something in my happiness, the fulfilment. I also felt overwhelmed from lots of new information about the world in addition to working long hours as an engineer. A new wish started to occur in me. I would love to have a laptop lifestyle.

Then I was invited to the first karma yoga practitioner training as a translator in Budapest. That was the first time I experienced the Samadhi meditation and got into the karma vortex. A couple of weeks later I knew I needed to move to London and be a healer. I kept my engineer work and informed my manager that I will work from London, and I will be available only through digital meetings from now on. This was back in 2018, prior to Covid-19. This is how my second wish of living a laptop lifestyle came true without being a digital marketer.

What I wanted to demonstrate here is that you can wish for anything even things which are totally against the norms of society like the 2 working day week. However, it may happen in an unexpected way rather than in a way you expected. My favourite quote is "Always expect the unexpected and whenever you can be the unexpected."

My advice here is to look at your life and analyze if it is aligned with your current desire. If yes that is amazing! If not make a list of what you would like to change, make the decision that you want that change and take the first step. Change something in your physical environment, in your relationships, in your attitude, in your appearance, in your health and you will see miracles start to happen. Just make that decision and take action. By being connected to your higher self, by not losing focus and not changing your wish for a new one, your wishes will be brought to you faster. The Universe needs time to arrange everything so the outcome of your wish won't leave anyone short. That is why we need to wait for the divine timing.

How to become the light?

CHAPTER

5

How to become the light

You are the light when people start to be drawn towards you and ask for your advice, when they feel peace around you and when they feel better after just connecting with you through words or just watching your video. When you are the light, you spread the light and people catch it and it heals them. Your light is "visible" from thousands of kilometres away. How can you reach that level and why is it important to become the light?

First of all, reading this book shows your intention to become a lightworker so you obviously want to become the light to help others. It is a long process; it takes sacrifice and hard work and lots of practise. I would start with meditation and learn energy healing techniques which allow your crown chakra to open wide, so you are able to invoke more energy/light from the Universe. It takes at least one year to go through the healing levels and practise the necessary healings on yourself first.

You will realize during the healings that your cravings and taste will also change. You will be more conscious about what you put into your body, how you use your body. You definitely will feel a need to change your diet for at least vegetarian, but better for a vegan diet. Meat carries all the pain and suffering of the animals on a cellular level and lowers your vibration when you eat them. Other products to consider quitting are alcohol, coffee, garlic and onion. Under the influence of alcohol, we tend to make different choices that could bring unwanted situations into our life and negative karma. Daily consumption of garlic and onion can lead to negative emotions such as anger, lethargy and morning depression and whilst they can support a healthy strong body, they are blocking the 6th sense due to their dominant fire element. Caffeine is a drug, a stimulus and it makes it difficult for the consciousness to rise. It lowers the life energy in the body.

By keeping a positive attitude towards others and towards the circumstances, your vibration will rise, and your light will be bigger too.

Let's look at food now which actually supports the activation of your pineal gland and your 3rd eye opening. Some of them might be well-known but I am sure you will also find some surprises. Cocoa was used for thousands of years in spiritual rituals to enhance the 6th sense. It contains a small amount of caffeine but also contains a large amount of theobromine which supports third eye opening. Basil and oregano are also amazing herbs for activating and decalcifying the pineal gland. But remember everything is only useful in moderation.

The Key

The Key

The key is to be an expert in your field, to provide the best service for others. Not to be the one called a scammer. People are looking at you as the key to the solution for their struggles. They trust you and they invest in you. They share their life and their deepest misery. They cry and laugh with you. You become an important point in their life in that moment. You need to respect them, to serve them through your highest knowledge. Your wisdom and comments can break them, lift them, save them or kill them. Although we know everyone is responsible for their own life, we need to be extremely conscious of what we teach and recommend to others. We are in a position of trust when we see their future and we need to provide them with the most encouraging positive advice. Since we are what we think and feel, it's better to feed others with only positive thoughts. That said, do not get engaged with the outcome of the results of your healings. This means do not worry about the client or feel responsibility towards them because that will create energy draining cords and will make you sick.

After learning the techniques, be patient with yourself while you are practising to become a master. Trust the process and that the Universe will bring you the people who need you at that stage and will also help you to exercise what you have learnt. Meditate daily and always pay attention to what comes up, all the images count. They are messages about yourself and your clients' past, current or future life connections. Ask help from the spirit guides and angels to gain more clarity in certain situations. When you step on this journey, you will take on duties which will be new and uncomfortable but also exciting and lifting experiences. You will feel fulfilled, and your self-esteem will grow. Also, you will realize your invincible supernatural traits. This encourages you even more to keep going on this path. Eventually you gain so much knowledge and power that you will literally fly around and spread your star dust on people.

Be the light

CHAPTER

7

Be the light

How to wear your power? After practising the meditations and going through healings you will feel healthier and stronger physically and also mentally which will empower you to believe in yourself. Morning affirmations and gratitude will also support your solar plexus chakra and keep your self-esteem and willpower higher. This is the point when you cannot allow others to stop you and remove you from this path. Because they will try to do that. Some low vibration people will feel destructed by your light and want to convince you to have a real job or spend more time with the family. They will start to use the blame game, to make you feel guilty and ashamed of spending time on your passion. You need to be strong enough and assure yourself about your vision and plans. Do not be discouraged when you set goals and your short-term goals don't succeed. It is part of learning, keep going towards your purpose. Pay attention to the supporters. Realize that you will lose friends and the circle of your family members will get smaller too but this is all part of the process. The people who leave you have low vibration and would negatively influence your elevation. So please feel grateful for the process.

Heal yourself

Heal yourself

We can best serve others when we are already healed. It is also a long process and depends how much healing we need. I started my healing through Reiki. I also completed many family constellation therapies to heal the issues of my ancestors. Then I learned source memory healing and I was able to release emotional traumas from my unconscious mind. I also use Samadhi meditation and ancestral defect meditation regularly to keep my vibration high and receive cellular level healing. I learned Sekhem healing too. Days before I went to the Sekhem healing course I started to eat raw food due to the effect of the energies and I continued for another 2 months whilst I was healing myself with the Sekhem signs. I also use crystals regularly for my healing.

There are many more natural ways to release blockages which can be of benefit. I have just listed those I personally use. The reason we need to do all these healings is to overcome self-sabotaging programming, to get rid of emotional traumas so we won't trigger them again and we won't eventually get physically or mentally sick from them.

I have talked so far about how to raise your frequency, but another important part of our well-being is to stay grounded. If we meditate too much or do other healings but we skip the grounding exercises we can have a foggy mind and could feel a bit moody, unstable, and insecure. The best way to ground yourself is to imagine that you are a tree and roots coming out of your palms, soles and from your root chakra towards the Earth and going to the centre of it. You can also say mantras like: "I am a human being and I belong to the Earth, and I am rooting myself to Mother Earth."

Other options for grounding are to take a shower or a bath, do some physical activity, exercise, eat and drink. Also, it's important to listen to our body and to the messages from our guides. Sometimes we get frustrated and sad when we are sick, we need to have patience for healing and ask for help from the other side. Actually, listen to your intuition and follow their advice.

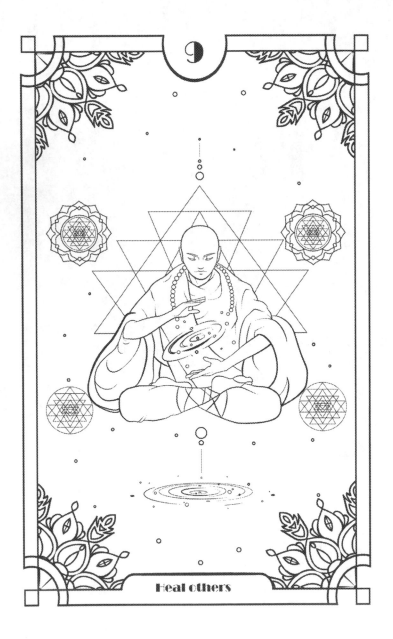

Heal others

Heal others

When you have the capability to perform healing, start healing others. It is a great chance to practise and also an amazing feeling to contribute to others' well-being. Firstly, offer free healings to your family members. You can actually heal your family members without asking for permission. When you start healing people outside your family you need to ask for permission first. They can also allow you to heal their relatives without informing the individual.

But there is an issue when the healer cannot communicate with the client directly and help them to change their mindset. Part of the healing is to lift up the client's mood, encourage them and inspire them to heal since their body will actually heal itself with the help of the universal energies.

When you send healing to someone, but you can't communicate with them directly they can actually ruin the effect of the healing spontaneously with their negative thinking. That is why it is really important to take time to speak with the client and support them mentally as well on their healing journey.

Self-care

Self-care

Fill your own cup before helping others. Self-care starts with setting boundaries so, you have space and you can breathe. At the beginning, it will take more time to train your environment, so they can perform activities without your supervision. That will allow you to schedule yourself a massage, bath ritual or daily meditation, without being constantly interrupted.

One of my friends just implemented "Momcation" into her life, which is an amazing tool for self-care taking a couple of days vacation with friends only and being away from the everyday responsibilities. Please do not feel guilty about it, as you know this kind of negative emotion can block your heart chakra. Just go all in and enjoy. Of course, it depends on the age of your kids and other circumstances. But make sure you find the way to release steam and be in different scenery. You do not need to party all night. Simply being out of your comfort zone literally and physically will help you to see yourself and your life in another perspective and also creates new neuron pathways in your brain with the new information and experiences that you invoke during the trip.

The knowing

The Knowing

When you start to surrender and the worry of the future dissolves, triggers of the past stop, you feel calmer and prefer to be in peace than to be right, that is the moment you are in the knowing. Knowing that you are one with everything, knowing that your plans will be achieved, knowing that you will be always loved, knowing that you love every living creature because separation is an illusion. When babies are born to this Earth, they don't know about separation; they have this knowing of the oneness with others. For months and years, they still believe they are part of their mom. They want to taste everything; invoke all the physical experiences and they also feel what their mother feels. That is why it's such a big responsibility to consciously be in a positive state by taking care of ourselves.

I still remember the day when I felt it for the first time. I was in my room after meditation, and I felt that inner peace and everlasting trust in the oneness. All my worries vanished away which had kept me stressed in those days for months. It was an uplifting feeling which stays forever. It would sometimes be lighter and sometimes stronger depending on my physical and mental state.

Spread the light

C H A P T E R

12

Spread the light

When you are the light, you need to understand that by simply being you, giving your time to others and just communicating with them, you are already healing them. You need to embody the new worth of yourself. Can you imagine how worthy you are just by being you and by connecting with others you are already spreading light? That is why the self-care is so important as well because you are continually connecting to people who are, most of the time, lower vibrational individuals, so you are in a position to lift them. However, you need to be conscious all the time not to get into their drama and – it might sounds a bit strange – but forget about being an empath. Lightworkers tend to be empaths and are very sensitive. Being an empath is dangerous; taking on all the negative feelings of others can seriously damage you. Use light protection every day.

Imagine that you create a beautiful light ball around you in the morning which is strong enough to hold back the negative energies and only the positive ones can go through it. Watch your feelings, watch your thoughts, and watch your words.

Manifest

Manifest

As high-vibrational people we are blessed with the capability to manifest our heart's desire. Most people manifest from their subconscious level which is full of fear and negative beliefs.

There are certain steps we can make to take full control of our manifestation.

Steps to manifest are the following: set the intention and focus on that, visualise that every morning and evening through emotions and feelings then let it go for the day and enjoy yourself to keep your vibration high all day. These are all the basics.

However what if your intention is not fully aligned with you? It is an idea of your environment or is it influenced by others? What if you still have subconscious blockages, fears that are protecting you from it happening?

If this is the case, the following steps are crucial before you manifest:

1. Take a break from life or life will force you to do so when you are off track of your purpose. When you feel like the manifestations are not happening just take a break and relax, spend time in nature, meditate, using energy healing modalities, emotional trauma clearing tools. Why is this necessary? Because then you will see where you went off track, what is really important to you and how you want to continue to live your life. Don't forget to manifest easily without struggle, it has to be aligned with you and you need to enjoy it.

2. Declutter what doesn't serve you anymore. As soon as you find out what is aligned and what is your true intention, start to get rid of everything that is not aligned and does not give you happiness and serve your purpose. Here comes the question of giving up. In our culture to give up is failure. If it is about your dream, you are totally aligned and vibrating highly, there is no such power that could force you to give up. If it is something that you picked to do because it seemed a good option or a temporary occupation or support but does not provide joy and happiness YOU NEED TO GIVE IT UP. Don't feel ashamed about it. This is your life and you need to keep your vibration high. If you do something which is not aligned with you and doesn't bring you joy,

stop it. If you can't give it up, you still have two options: outsource that activity or change your perspective about it and start to enjoy it. You can control your emotions so you can change your state of being. But be careful, because in that case it will delay your real dreams. It will delay the manifestation of your heart's desire because energy flows where focus goes.

3. Be a yes man! After finding clarity and decluttering the things that don't serve you, allow the energies to flow and be ready to receive. Be with open eyes, an open heart and open arms. Be able to see the new opportunities and the new connections. The Universe or God brings your manifestation through people and opportunities.

4. When you receive your manifestation, nourish it to flourish! When we receive our manifestations, we tend to feel blessed and overflow with gratitude at first but then we sit back. Because we think we are done. NO! This is the next phase: you show your appreciation by nurturing it, loving it and growing it. When you take care of your manifestation through unconditional love, new manifestations will pop up and grow like mushrooms in the forest after the rain. And your life will change dramatically for the best.

What should you do if you happened to manifest something which seemed a good idea at first but then turned out to be a bad experience?

First of all, do not feel guilty or ashamed about it because that will block your heart chakra. Secondly, ask for forgiveness from God and forgive yourself. Then make sure you appreciate the lesson by taking action to give up the situation. As I said it's not failure to give up something that doesn't align with you. It gives you back control of your life. Sometimes even when we make conscious decisions but do not bring in our gut feeling, it still could have negative consequences, heartbreak, pain and suffering. So, every decision needs to be checked in the following ways. Am I aligned with this? Is it supported by my higher self? Is it aligned with my mission, how will it affect my life and my circumstances? Will it jeopardise me or my loved ones? When all are properly answered you can manifest it.

About the Author

Edit B Kiss is a holistic mentor, success habit coach, writer, #1 bestselling author, Humanitarian Award winner and international speaker. She helps leaders to get healed from running mind, insomnia to gain more focus and fill the void in their hearts by raising their frequency and getting them aligned with their true self so they can stand the storms and live their life joyfully and reinvent themselves to the next level.

She worked with clients on releasing long-lasting pains, blockages, ancestor defects and emotional traumas so they could live fulfil and joyful lives. She has clients from all over the world, including the United States, New Zealand, the United Kingdom, Hungary, and Nigeria; these range from millionaire traders to influencers to artists.

She was the subject of a one-hour interview on Deborah Funmi Mupapa's "Life Assurance" podcast in which she discussed life, marriage, and soul. She was also featured on the "On the Edge with April Mahoney" podcast. She was a key presenter and panelist on "Global Hope Conference" in the topic of Covid-19 pandemic.

"Authority Magazine" published her advices about the 5 Ways to Develop Serenity during Anxious Time. She is a co-author of the #1 bestseller "1 Habit for Entrepreneurial Success" with Forbes Riley and others. Thrive Global called her the Habit Expert, promoting her "5 Things You Need to Create Good Habits" video with her interview. She is also a co-author of the book "Soul Food" with Amy Elizabeth. She has been interviewed in the "Business Innovators Radio" by Mark Pooler. She also helped with healing ideas in the "Tiaras Tears and Triumphs Podcast" by Sandy J from Australia.

Edit originally was a petroleum engineer, working in the petroleum industry for 15 years before being a life-coach full time. During those years she trained to become a Reiki Master, a Sekhem Healer and a Karma Yogi Practitioner under the teaching of Karma Guru Sumant Kaul; strengthened her extra senses; and worked on several family constellation therapies. She learned life-coaching from the Satori Prime brothers (who base their work on Landmark approaches) and was trained by Bob Proctor, who is known for his appearance as a featured expert in the movie, The Secret. While living in New Zealand, she was a member of Reiki NZ Incorporated healing for free.

Check out the following website for more information: editbkiss.com

Printed in the United States
by Baker & Taylor Publisher Services